I say hello to my cousins Kieran, Haresh and Ricky and their dog Rex. I would love to have a dog too, but we can't because animal fur can give me a reaction called **eczema** that makes my skin itch.

OTHER ALLERGIES

Children with food allergies often have other conditions such as **asthma** and **eczema**.

I love quad bikes and we always have a great time playing on them at Kieran's house. Rex wants to join in too!

Mum and Aunty Kally are checking the food in the kitchen. They read all the labels to make sure nothing contains nuts or traces of nuts. They have to check everything, like the bread for the burgers, biscuits, and cakes.

I have a big family! My granddad and grandma are at the party, as well as my mum and dad, aunt and uncle and cousins. There is lots of food for us to eat.

There are some special Asian dishes like **lentil** curry and ludu, which are sweets made from flour, sugar and milk. Mum reminds me that these dishes might have nuts in them.

19

I'm sitting next to my friend Joshua. We're in the same class at school. Joshua has food allergies too. He can't eat the lentil curry because he's allergic to lentils.

The foods that most often cause allergies include milk, eggs, nuts, wheat, fish, shell fish and soy beans.

Joshua has brought a big birthday present to the party for Kieran. Kieran loves getting presents!

It's time for Kieran to cut the cake! He blows out the candles first. It's a sponge cake. Mum has checked that it has no nuts in it, so it's okay for me to eat.

Aunty Kally is giving me, Joshua and Sanjay party bags to take home. They have little toys and sweets in them. I can't wait to look in mine!

It's been a great party but it's time to go home now. We say goodbye to Aunty Kally and to our cousins.

When we get home, Sanjay and I look in our party bags. I got a chocolate bar that might have nuts in it, so Mum tells me to swop with Sanjay. His chocolate bar is safe for me to eat.

The worst thing about having a food allergy is that you can't always eat what everyone else is eating. Sometimes I have to miss a party if we don't know what the food will be like. Mum or Dad stay at home with me.

But there are lots of foods I enjoy that are safe for me to eat. One of my favourites is homemade pizza!

Glossary

Adrenaline a medicine which helps to calm allergic reactions, making it easier to breathe

Asthma a condition that causes problems with breathing. It can be an allergy

Eczema a condition that causes a rash and itching. It can be an allergy

Food allergy when the body reacts badly to food that is harmless for most people

Injection having a prick from a needle to put something into our body

Lentil a kind of plant seed which is eaten as a vegetable

Index

Further Information

UNITED KINGDOM
The Anaphylaxis Campaign
Tel. 01252 542029
www.anaphylaxis.org.uk
Information and guidance for people with the severe food allergy called anaphylaxis. A range of educational products, including information sheets and videos are available.

Allergy UK
Tel: 020 8303 8525
www.allergyfoundation.com
Up-to-date information, advice and support for people with allergies. Information fact sheets are available.

UNITED STATES OF AMERICA
The Food Allergy and Anaphylaxis Network
Resources and support for allergy sufferers, as well as tips on how to manage food allergies.

AUSTRALIA
Food Anaphylactic Children Training and Support Association (FACTS)
Tel: 1300 728 000
www.allergyfacts.org.au
Practical help for food allergy sufferers.

NEW ZEALAND
Allergy New Zealand Inc
Tel: 0800 34 0800
www.allergy.org.nz
Education and information for allergy sufferers.

BOOKS
Allergies (Health Matters), Carol Baldwin, Heinemann Library 2002

Birthday Party: Meet Alexandra who has a Food Allergy, Dianne Church, Franklin Watts 2003

Let's Talk about Having Allergies, Elisabeth Weitzman, Powerkids Press 2003

Why Do My Eyes Itch? And Other Questions About Allergies (Body Matters)
Angela Royston, Heinemann Library 2003